BATSWANA

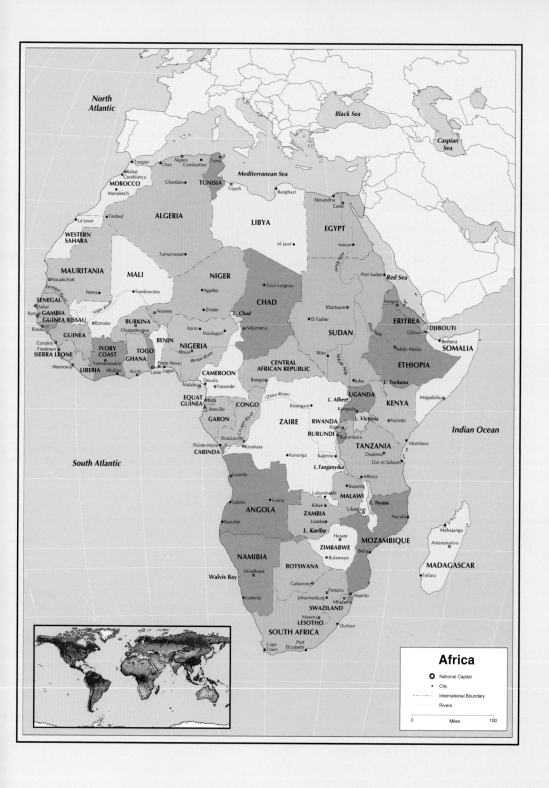

North
Atlantic

Black Sea

Caspian
Sea

Mediterranean Sea

MOROCCO
Tangier
Rabat
Casablanca
Marrakech
La'youn
Tindouf

Algiers
Oran
Constantine
Tunis
Ghardaia
TUNISIA
Tripoli
Banghazi
Alexandria
Cairo

WESTERN
SAHARA

ALGERIA

LIBYA

Al Jawf

EGYPT

Aswan

MAURITANIA
Nouakchott
Nema

MALI

Tamanrasset

NIGER
Agadez

CHAD
Faya-Largeau

Port Sudan
Red Sea

Asmera
ERITREA
DJIBOUTI
Djibouti
Berbera
SOMALIA

SENEGAL
Dakar
GAMBIA
Banjul
GUINEA BISSAU
Bissau
GUINEA
Conakry
Freetown
SIERRA LEONE
Monrovia
LIBERIA

Tombouctou

Niamey
Zinder
L. Chad

Bamako
Ouagadougou
BURKINA
Kano
Maidugure
Ndjamena

El Fasher

Khartoum

SUDAN

Blue Nile

Addis Ababa
ETHIOPIA

IVORY
COAST
Yamoussoukro
Abidjan
Accra

BENIN
NIGERIA
Abuja
Benue River
Porto Novo
Lome Lagos

TOGO
GHANA

CAMEROON
Douala
Malabo
Yaounde
EQUAT.
GUINEA
Bata
Libreville

CONGO

GABON

CENTRAL
AFRICAN REPUBLIC

Bangui

(Zaire River)

Wau

White Nile

Juba

UGANDA
Kisangani
L. Albert
Kampala

Mogadishu

L. Turkana

KENYA
Nairobi

Indian Ocean

South Atlantic

Congo River

Brazzaville
Pointe-Noire
Kinshasa
CABINDA

ZAIRE

RWANDA
Kigali
BURUNDI
Bujumbura
L. Victoria

TANZANIA
Dodoma
Dar es Salaam
Mombasa

Kananga

Kalemie

L.Tanganyika

Luanda

Lobito
Luena

ANGOLA
Namibe

Lubumbashi
Kasama
MALAWI
Kitwe
Lilongwe
L. Nyasa

ZAMBIA
Lusaka
L. Kariba

Mbeya

Nacala

Walvis Bay

NAMIBIA
Windhoek

BOTSWANA

Gaborone

Luderitz

Harare
Bulawayo
ZIMBABWE
Beira

MOZAMBIQUE

Mahajanga
Antananarivo

MADAGASCAR
Toliara

Pretoria
Johannesburg
Mbabane
Maputo
SWAZILAND
Maseru
LESOTHO
Durban

SOUTH AFRICA
Cape
Town
Port
Elizabeth

The Heritage Library of African Peoples

BATSWANA

Maitseo Bolaane and
Part T. Mgadla, Ph.D.

THE ROSEN PUBLISHING GROUP, INC.
NEW YORK

Published in 1997 by The Rosen Publishing Group, Inc.
29 East 21st Street, New York, NY 10010

First Edition

Manufactured in the United States of America

Library of Congress Cataloging-in-Publication Data

Bolaane, Maitseo.
   Batswana / Maitseo Bolaane and Part T. Mgadla. — 1st ed.
      p.   cm. — (Heritage library of African peoples)
   Includes bibliographical references and index.
   Summary: Surveys the history, culture, and contemporary life of the Batswana people of Botswana and South Africa.
   ISBN 0-8239-2008-9
   1. Tswana (African people)—History—Juvenile literature.
2. Tswana (African people)—Social life and customs—Juvenile
literature.   3. Botswana—History—Juvenile literature.   [1. Tswana
(African people)]   I. Mgadla, Part Themba, 1953- .   II. Title.
III. Series.
DT2458.T89B65   1997
968.83—dc21   96-50255
                                                                CIP
                                                                 AC

Contents

Introduction   6

1. The Land and the People   9

2. History   19

3. Government and Economy   34

4. Religion and Customs   42

5. Botswana Today   56

    Glossary   61

    For Further Reading   62

    Index   63

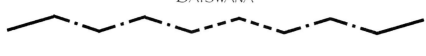

INTRODUCTION

THERE IS EVERY REASON FOR US TO KNOW something about Africa and to understand its past and the way of life of its peoples. Africa is a rich continent that has for centuries provided the world with art, culture, labor, wealth, and natural resources. It has vast mineral deposits, fossil fuels, and commercial crops.

But perhaps most important is the fact that fossil evidence indicates that human beings originated in Africa. The earliest traces of human beings and their tools are almost two million years old. Their descendants have migrated throughout the world. To be human is to be of African descent.

The experiences of the peoples who stayed in Africa are as rich and as diverse as of those who established themselves elsewhere. This series of books describes their environment, their modes of subsistence, their relationships, and their customs and beliefs. The books present the variety of languages, histories, cultures, and religions that are to be found on the African continent. They demonstrate the historical linkages between African peoples and the way contemporary Africa has been affected by European colonial rule.

Africa is large, complex, and diverse. It encompasses an area of more than 11,700,000 square miles. The United States, Europe, and India could fit easily into it. The sheer size is an indication of the continent's great variety in geography, terrain, climate, flora, fauna, peoples, languages, and cultures.

Much of contemporary Africa has been shaped by European colonial rule, industrialization, urbanization, and the demands of a world economic system. For more than seventy years, large regions of Africa were ruled by Great Britain, France, Belgium, Portugal, and Spain. African peoples from various ethnic, linguistic, and cultural backgrounds were brought together to form colonial states.

For decades Africans struggled to gain their independence. It was not until after World War II that the colonial territories became independent African states. Today, almost all of Africa is ruled by Africans. Large numbers of Africans live in modern cities. Rural Africa is also being transformed, and yet its people still engage in many of their customs and beliefs.

Contemporary circumstances and natural events have not always been kind to ordinary Africans. Today, however, new popular social movements and technological innovations pose great promise for future development.

George C. Bond, Ph.D., Director
Institute of African Studies
Columbia University, New York

Batswana, meaning the Tswana people, live in both South Africa and Botswana.
This elderly woman is a guest at a rural wedding. Her formal dress includes a head
scarf and a blanket. She holds a gourd cup containing nutritious traditional beer,
which is made from grain.

chapter

1

THE LAND AND
THE PEOPLE

BATSWANA LIVE IN THE COUNTRIES OF
Botswana and South Africa. Until South Africa's
apartheid system of racial discrimination
was abandoned in 1994, many Batswana in
South Africa lived in the ethnic homeland of
Bophuthatswana. Bophuthatswana was located
in what is today the Northwest Province of
South Africa. This book focuses on the Batswana
in Botswana. About half of Botswana's population lives in small villages, each containing less
than 5,000 people.

Batswana speak a language called Setswana.
Setswana has several different dialects, but
Batswana from different regions can understand
each other because the dialects are closely re-
lated. Anything that is regarded as an essential
part of the culture of Batswana is also called
Setswana. For example, one might refer to
Batswana customs as Setswana customs.

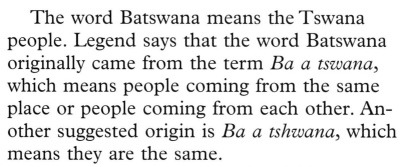

The word Batswana means the Tswana people. Legend says that the word Batswana originally came from the term *Ba a tswana,* which means people coming from the same place or people coming from each other. Another suggested origin is *Ba a tshwana,* which means they are the same.

In Setswana and many other African languages, the prefix *ba-* means "the." The English names of many African peoples often replace *ba-* with "the." Therefore, Batswana are often called the Tswana in English. In practice, the people are also often called "the Batswana," although this version of the name repeats both the prefix *ba-* and its English equivalent, "the."

Botswana is bordered by South Africa in the south and southeast, Namibia in the west, and Zimbabwe in the northeast. It also touches Zambia in the north. Botswana is roughly the size of the state of Texas in the United States. Although Botswana covers a large area, it is one of the least populated countries in the world. Its population in 1991 was 1.3 million people.

Roughly 3 million Batswana live in South Africa. The Batswana in Botswana and South Africa were separated in the 1800s, when colonial borders were established by white settlers. At that time Botswana was under British rule and was called the Bechuanaland Protectorate.

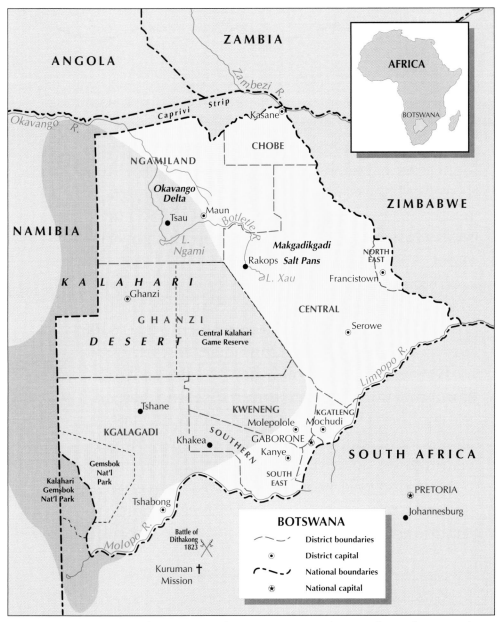

ZAMBIA

ANGOLA

AFRICA

BOTSWANA

Zambezi R.

Okavango R.

Caprivi Strip

Kasane

CHOBE

NGAMILAND

Okavango Delta

Tsau

Maun

Botletle R.

ZIMBABWE

NAMIBIA

L. Ngami

Makgadikgadi

Rakops **Salt Pans**

NORTH EAST

L. Xau

Francistown

K A L A H A R I

Ghanzi

G H A N Z I

CENTRAL

Serowe

D E S E R T

Central Kalahari Game Reserve

Limpopo R.

Tshane

KWENENG

KGATLENG

Molepolole

Mochudi

KGALAGADI

Khakea

SOUTHERN

GABORONE

Kanye

SOUTH AFRICA

Gemsbok Nat'l Park

SOUTH EAST

Kalahari Gemsbok Nat'l Park

Tshabong

PRETORIA

Johannesburg

Molopo R.

Battle of Dithakong 1823

Kuruman † Mission

BOTSWANA

- - - District boundaries
- ⊙ District capital
- ⌐-- National boundaries
- ⊛ National capital

Batswana make up the majority of Botswana's population of 1.3 million people. Today Botswana includes much of the territory that Batswana have occupied for many centuries. However, roughly 3 million Batswana live in neighboring South Africa. There they are found mainly in the large cities, such as Johannesburg, and in the areas close to the Botswana border. Until 1994 many of these Batswana in South Africa were forced to live in a homeland, or reservation, called Bophuthatswana. When South Africa abolished apartheid and became a democratic country in 1994, the homelands ceased to exist.

▼ GOVERNMENT ▼

Botswana became independent from Great Britain in 1966. Today Botswana is one of the few African countries that is a multiparty democracy, based on the British parliamentary system. This system allows several political parties to exist and compete fairly. The party that wins the most votes controls the government.

Elections in Botswana are held every five years. Seven political parties competed in the 1994 elections. The Botswana Democratic Party has won all of the elections held so far.

Botswana's parliamentary system protects human rights and free enterprise and has an independent system of justice. People can own and operate businesses. The laws prevent discrimination against minorities. Many Batswana believe that this modern system of government is firmly rooted in their ancient democratic traditions.

▼ THE LAND ▼

Two-thirds of Botswana is desert or semiarid. This is because the Kgalagadi, or Kalahari Desert, comprises a large part of the country. The population is concentrated in the more fertile eastern part of the country.

Botswana usually gets between eighteen and twenty-seven inches of rainfall each year. But

Botswana is a country of great contrasts. The western part is dominated by the Kalahari Desert (top). The Okavango Delta region (bottom) in the northwest is crisscrossed with a network of rivers and experiences seasonal flooding.

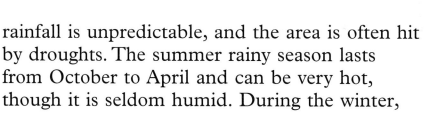

rainfall is unpredictable, and the area is often hit by droughts. The summer rainy season lasts from October to April and can be very hot, though it is seldom humid. During the winter, temperatures often drop below freezing at night (particularly in the southern part of the country), resulting in many frosty mornings.

▼ THE PEOPLE ▼

The Batswana creation story states that the people originated from an ancestor called Matsieng, or Lowe. He emerged from the underworld, bringing cattle, sheep, and goats. It is said that the prehistoric footprints found on some rocks in Botswana are from this ancient ancestor. The most famous footprint in stone is in Rasesa, a village twenty-five miles from Gaborone, the capital of Botswana.

Experts believe that the African peoples now living south of the Sahara Desert spread out across much of the continent over many centuries. Many of those who migrated into southern Africa consisted of related Sotho-Tswana peoples, of which the Batswana of today formed a part. Other major sections of this group include the South Sotho, or Basotho, and the North Sotho, or Bapedi.

Batswana are also sometimes called the Western Sotho. It is thought that the first Batswana peoples arrived in southern Africa between 1,000 and 2,000 years ago. The earliest Batswana groups were pushed westward into arid regions by stronger Batswana groups. In the 1800s Batswana peoples came under further pressure as whites and other African groups invaded their territory.

▼ *MERAFE* ▼

The Batswana peoples, in fact, consist of several subgroups called *merafe* (singular: *morafe*). A *morafe,* or chiefdom, consists of people descended from the same ancestor. Over many generations the *merafe* split into several branches. Often this occurred because of disputes between a chief's sons about who would succeed their father. Chiefs' sons or leading men broke away from the *morafe* with their followers and established their own independent *morafe.*

It is thought that through this process, the senior Bahurutshe *morafe* gave rise to other *merafe*: the Bakwena, Bangwato, Bangwaketse, Batawana, Bakgatla, and Batlharo. Other important *merafe* are the Barolong and the Batlhaping. Today the Bangwato are the largest group in Botswana and occupy the most land.

Merafe can be identified by the totems that they honor. Totems are usually animals that serve as emblems for groups of people with the same origin or ancestry. People never kill, eat,

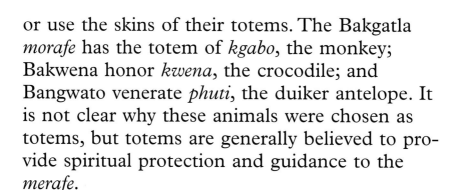

or use the skins of their totems. The Bakgatla *morafe* has the totem of *kgabo*, the monkey; Bakwena honor *kwena*, the crocodile; and Bangwato venerate *phuti*, the duiker antelope. It is not clear why these animals were chosen as totems, but totems are generally believed to provide spiritual protection and guidance to the *merafe*.

▼ WAY OF LIFE ▼

The common language of Setswana unites all Batswana *merafe*. Most of them also share a similar traditional way of life, which consists of three key elements: cattle, farming, and village life. Batswana families traditionally live in a village, or *motse*. Daily activities include the plowing of lands and the rearing of cattle, which are kept at an outlying cattle post, or *moraka*.

Most rural families' wealth and status are measured by the size of their cattle herds. A few cattle are brought in from the *moraka* to pull plows during the planting season, usually between November and January. Cattle are also sometimes brought to the village to be sold to other big cattle ranchers or to the slaughterhouse. Beef is consumed locally and exported to foreign countries, such as England and Belgium.

Today, of course, many Batswana are involved in professional and technical occupations in

In the past, cattle were the cornerstone of Batswana society and the economy. Today many rural Batswana families still keep cattle herds (above), and large companies also run vast cattle ranches. Cattle therefore continue to play a vital role in the economy of modern Botswana.

southern Africa and other parts of the world. Botswana is a developing country with many mineral resources. It has one of the most successful economies in Africa. However, the income of rural people is generally very low.

Batswana once lived in round houses that were made of mud and thatched with grass. Three or four houses made up a family homestead. A Batswana community, or *motse*,

17

In rural areas, a Batswana family homestead consists of several separate structures. This woman uses a grass broom to sweep the area outside her kitchen, which is seen in the background.

consisted of hundreds and sometimes thousands of these homesteads.

In recent times, houses have been influenced by Western architecture, and modern cities have been built. However, traditional houses are still seen in rural areas. The idea of the *motse* as a united community remains important to many Batswana today.▲

chapter

2

HISTORY

FROM THE LATE 1400S ON, TRADERS FROM various European countries sailed around the southern tip of the African continent to trade with Asian countries.

▼ FIRST CONTACT WITH EUROPEANS ▼
Batswana were largely unaffected by the arrival of the Portuguese, the first Europeans to visit the coast of southern Africa. The Dutch established the first European settlement in southern Africa at Cape Town in 1652. In 1806 Britain took control of the Cape Colony.

During the 1800s and much of the 1900s, white colonials of Dutch and British background competed for control not only of the Cape Colony, but for the whole of southern Africa. This competition had a great impact on Batswana history. At first, African people in the

19

WILDLIFE

For centuries Batswana hunted and managed their wildlife without outside interference. Chiefs controlled the hunting of animals. They maintained a healthy balance between respecting wildlife and meeting the needs of the people to hunt for meat, grow crops, and graze livestock.

Today almost 25 percent of Botswana's land surface area is divided into wildlife management areas. These are reserves where the local communities have a say in how to manage the wild animals that live in their area.

Botswana's unique wildlife habitats include the sand dunes of the Kalahari Desert, the inland swamps of the Okavango Delta, and a number of dry salt pans, such as the Makgadikgadi Pans. About 17 percent of Botswana's land is protected wilderness and has rich animal life. Favorites with tourists are lions, leopards, elephants, buffalos, and rhinos. Also found are a wide variety of antelopes, including the eland, kudu, duiker, and sable, and hundreds of species of beautiful birds.

As a result of the way Botswana has managed its wildlife and natural environment, it is now one of the world's most popular countries for ecotourism, or tourism that focuses on the natural environment.

region met with European missionaries and traders. These missionaries and traders, however, were usually followed by colonial administrators and military forces, which sought to control native populations.

▼ DIFAQANE ▼

In the early 1800s several African societies began to experience dramatic social changes.

These were caused by several reasons. After a long period of good climate and prosperity, several groups had grown considerably. A shortage of grazing land led to competition between groups. At the same time, whites had established trading centers on the coast, and African groups competed to control profitable trade routes to and from the coast.

Shaka, king of the Zulu, came to dominate most of eastern South Africa. A ruthless conqueror, he forced neighboring chiefs to accept his authority or flee. Even some of Shaka's most powerful generals, such as Mzilikazi of the Ndebele, deserted Shaka. As these groups fled Zululand, they were forced to attack the people they encountered on their path in order to obtain cattle and grain for food. In turn, those who lost their food stores to attackers had no option but to attack their own neighbors. The chain reaction plunged southern Africa into chaos. This terrible time of starvation and violence is known as the Difaqane, which means the time of great troubles. (In Zulu it is called Mfecane.)

▼ MISSIONARIES ▼

The first European missionary to settle among the Setswana-speaking peoples was Robert Moffat, who belonged to the London Missionary Society (LMS). He settled at Kuruman among the

This picture of a Batlhaping chief and his wife was drawn by John Campbell, who visited Kuruman in the early 1820s.

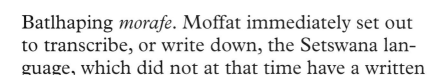

Batlhaping *morafe*. Moffat immediately set out to transcribe, or write down, the Setswana language, which did not at that time have a written form.

In 1823 the Batlhaping town of Dithakong was attacked by a large army of starving refugees from the south. The army consisted largely of South Sotho peoples who were distant relatives of the Batswana groups. Moffat called for urgent assistance from the Griquas, a frontier people who were largely of Khoekhoe background. At the famous battle of Dithakong, 100 Griqua horsemen with firearms and 1,000 Batlhaping easily drove off the much larger attacking army, which did not have any guns.

The ability of missionaries to organize and protect the people with whom they lived and worked encouraged African chiefs to accept missionaries. Another important LMS missionary was David Livingstone, the famous explorer, who lived among Bakwena for a time. Moffat, Livingstone, and other missionaries attempted to promote peace among competing African groups during the Difaqane.

Moffat, in particular, developed a relationship with Mzilikazi, who was the most feared and powerful leader in the Batswana region. This friendship did not, however, prevent Mzilikazi from attacking Batswana groups. In 1832 he defeated the Bahurutshe subgroup. Their chief

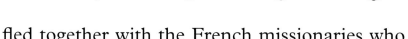

fled together with the French missionaries who were living among his people.

Working closely with Batswana chiefs, or *dikgosi* (singular: *kgosi*), missionaries introduced aspects of Western culture. Besides plows, wagons, and other Western articles, they also introduced Christianity and Western-style education. As a result, many Batswana customs changed.

▼ BOERS AND BRITONS ▼

The British introduced several reforms after they took control of the Cape Colony from the Dutch. They abolished slavery, introduced a stronger and fairer judicial system, and limited the Boers' ability to take over land belonging to African peoples.

Many African groups were weakened or displaced from their land shortly before settlers of Dutch background, called Boers (farmers) or Afrikaners (after their language of Afrikaans), began to enter the interior of South Africa.

The Boers wanted to establish their own republics to the north and east of the coastal areas under British control. The most important republics became the Transvaal and the Orange Free State, both in South Africa. Both of these republics were established by forcefully taking land that belonged to Africans.

Boers in the western Transvaal (now the Northwest Province of South Africa) constantly threatened to take over Batswana land. This alarmed both Batswana and the missionaries of the LMS, including Moffat and Livingstone. In 1852 Livingstone helped the Bakwena repel a Boer attack at the Battle of Dimawe.

The British were eager to limit Boer expansion. They feared that the Germans, who occupied South-West Africa (Namibia), would also move into Batswana lands. If the Germans and the Boers united, they could block British plans to expand northward themselves.

The Boers exploited tensions between Batswana chiefs and used the conflict to their own advantage. They took grazing land belonging to Barolong under Chief Montshioa and brought these Barolong under their authority. This move threatened the Missionary Road, the route that travelers from South Africa took to the north.

To protect the Missionary Road, in 1885 the British placed the Barolong territory under their control as British Bechuanaland. Much of this land later became the South African homeland of Bophuthatswana. The remainder of Batswana territory was also placed under British protection. Called the Bechuanaland Protectorate, it remained under British control until it became Botswana in 1966.

▼ THE BRITISH SOUTH AFRICA ▼
COMPANY

In 1895 the Batswana were faced with another threat: Cecil Rhodes's British South

Africa Company (BSAC). Cecil Rhodes was a
British financier who had made millions from
the diamond mines in South Africa. He ambi-
tiously planned to extend the British Empire
until it crossed Africa from Cape Town to Cairo,
Egypt, preferably under his control. He formed
the BSAC to exploit the resources of African territories and govern these areas with the blessing
of the British crown.

Rhodes took over the country that became
present-day Zimbabwe by tricking Mzilikazi's
son, Lobengula, into signing over control.
He persuaded the British government to
let the BSAC take over the Bechuanaland
Protectorate for two reasons. First, he con-
vinced them that they could save money by
letting the BSAC take over the costs of running
the protectorate. Second, he argued that the
country had little value, since it was two-thirds
desert.

The chiefs of the Batswana strongly opposed
Cecil Rhodes and his plans for the land. In
1895, with the help of the LMS, three Batswana
dikgosi, or chiefs, went to London to protest.
They were Kgama III of Bangwato, Bathoeng
I of Bangwaketse, and Sebele of Bakwena. They
were able to retain most of Batswana territory.

Rhodes was disgraced in Britain when he
unsuccessfully attempted to overthrow the Boer
Republic of the Transvaal in order to seize

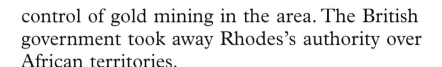

control of gold mining in the area. The British government took away Rhodes's authority over African territories.

▼ BRITISH ADMINISTRATION ▼

Although the Bechuanaland Protectorate was meant to be administered by Batswana themselves, the British gradually tightened their control. In 1891, for example, they set up an administration for the colony. Bechuanaland was governed by a high commissioner, who lived hundreds of miles away in Cape Town. A resident commissioner was stationed at Mafikeng. He oversaw a network of district commissioners and magistrates. They governed in association with the *dikgosi*, but ultimately served to undermine the powers of the *dikgosi*. Chiefs could no longer pass laws and exercise complete authority. They became employees of the colonial administration and had to collect taxes from their people to pay the British.

▼ BATSWANA REACTION ▼

Batswana, particularly the chiefs, were very outspoken in rejecting the interference by British colonial authority. In 1920 the African Advisory Council (AAC) was formed to address some of the concerns of Batswana. Chiefs also used the AAC to resist British plans to hand over Bechuanaland to South African control. In the

SOL PLAATJE (1876–1932)

Solomon T. Plaatje (pronounced ply-KEY) is considered one of the most important and influential early African writers. His family, members of the Barolong *morafe*, had fled the Ndebele under Mzilikazi. His family name, Mhudi, was too difficult to pronounce for the Griqua people, with whom Plaatje's family settled at Bethanie Mission, so they were called Plaatje, which means flat head.

Sol Plaatje attended a mission school, which provided only five years of schooling. Recognizing his intelligence and motivation, the teacher's wife taught him English, German, and music, and lent him books. However, like many of the emerging elite of educated Africans, Plaatje was largely self-taught. Throughout his life, Plaatje encouraged his own people to take pride in their language and culture. He was also an African nationalist; he believed that black people should unite, despite their ethnic differences, to fight for their rights. He married a Xhosa-speaking woman against initial opposition from both their families, proving that he practiced what he preached.

Plaatje recorded the famous Siege of Mafikeng in his book *The Boer War Diary of Sol Plaatje*. Mafikeng, controlled by the British, was besieged by the Boers in 1899. Sol Plaatje provided a black man's view of the war between the settlers and described the plight of the 10,000 blacks besieged in Mafikeng. His book *Mhudi* was the first novel written in English by a southern African black writer. Based on the historic conflict between the Ndebele and Barolong, the novel credits the leaders' wives for bringing about peace. Plaatje studied Shakespeare, whose works he translated into Setswana. He also recorded Setswana oral literature, such as folktales and legends, and African music.

Plaatje was a critic of colonialism and racism. He expressed his views in the newspapers he founded. He also helped organize the South African Native National Congress, which preceded the African National Congress, the political movement that led South Africa to democracy. His other famous book, *Native Life in South Africa*, details the ways that blacks were forced off their land as a result of the Native Land Act of 1913. He wrote it in England, where he had gone to protest conditions in South Africa. He also traveled to the United States and Canada, giving speeches and doing research.

After his return to South Africa in 1923, Plaatje worked to improve conditions for urban blacks. In 1931 he traveled to the Belgian Congo on a fact-finding mission and took many photographs of the oppression black peoples there suffered under the Belgians.

Plaatje died of pneumonia in Johannesburg in 1932.

Plaatje is remembered for his important role in informing the world of the conditions under which blacks suffered during colonialism, for his role in politics, and for his literary achievements. Today many schools and streets in South Africa are named after Sol Plaatje. There is also a literary award named in his honor.

1930s the *dikgosi* used the AAC to combat British attempts to reduce the power of chiefs.

When World War II broke out, the British eased their effort to squash the power of the chiefs, because they needed the chiefs to encourage their men to enlist. Power was restored to the chiefs, but they continued to work closely with British authorities.

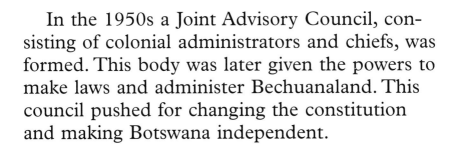

In the 1950s a Joint Advisory Council, consisting of colonial administrators and chiefs, was formed. This body was later given the powers to make laws and administer Bechuanaland. This council pushed for changing the constitution and making Botswana independent.

▼ RECENT HISTORY ▼

Since its independence in 1966, Botswana has faced tough challenges, particularly from its powerful neighbor, South Africa. Until 1994 South Africa was ruled by a racist apartheid government. Black people in South Africa had no vote, and the vast majority were forced by the white government to live in ethnic reservations called homelands.

In reality, these homelands had nothing to do with the true idea of home, since ethnic groups were frequently forced off land that they had called home for centuries. They were generally given inferior lands that the white rulers did not want. In this way, black people—87 percent of the population of South Africa—were allocated only 13 percent of the land.

The homelands divided black people according to their ethnic group, language, and culture. There were different homelands for the Tswana, Xhosa, Zulu, and many other groups. The homeland for Batswana in South Africa, called Bophuthatswana, bordered on Botswana. Led by

Chiefs continue to play an important role in both local and national affairs. Here a chief (standing) holds a community meeting, or *kgotla*, under the shade of the largest tree in the village.

Chief Lucas Mangope and supported by South Africa, Bophuthatswana claimed to be an independent country.

The white government of South Africa hoped that dividing the black population in this way would increase competition between black ethnic groups and prevent unity. This strategy failed. Black people's shared opposition to this racist system brought them together and led to the eventual collapse of the apartheid regime. Led by President Nelson Mandela, South Africa is now a free and democratic country. The homelands have now been dissolved.

31

Until 1994 Botswana's relationship with
South Africa was difficult because of the large
number of Batswana living within South Africa.
The residents of Botswana, along with people
from around the world, never recognized the
independence of the homelands and did not
support apartheid. But Botswana is economically
dependent on South Africa in several ways.
Botswana is a landlocked country, without ports
for international trade. Therefore, it must use
South African trade routes and ports. Botswana broke off diplomatic ties with South
Africa because of apartheid, but it had to
continue to trade with South Africa and
Bophuthatswana.

Until 1980 Zimbabwe, Batswana's neighbor
to the northeast, was also a white-dominated
country under the racist regime of Ian Smith.
This caused similar problems for Botswana,
which used Zimbabwe's railroads but did
not condone its politics. During the long
Zimbabwean war of independence, many
Batswana along the Zimbabwean border lost
their property or their lives.

In addition, South Africa ruled neighboring
Namibia until 1990. A war of independence was
fought in Namibia and along the Angolan border. Botswana had to deal with political exiles
and refugees from South Africa, Zimbabwe,
Namibia, and Angola. A large refugee center had

Donkey carts are an important means of transport for rural families, who often have to travel long distances to obtain supplies or sell their surplus produce.

to be built, and Botswana was continually threatened by its oppressive, white-ruled neighboring countries. At times South Africa invaded Botswana and killed exiles, political figures, and innocent people.

Today white rule in all of southern Africa has come to an end. Everyone now hopes that the region can develop and move forward in a peaceful and democratic manner.▲

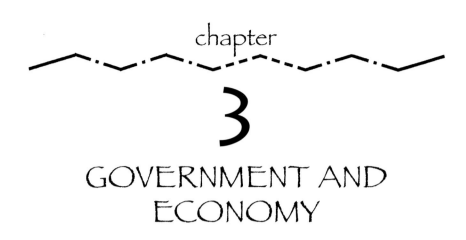

chapter
3

GOVERNMENT AND ECONOMY

BEFORE CONTACT WITH EUROPEAN TRADERS and missionaries, Batswana had their own system of government, economy, and social organization.

▼ *DIKGOSI* (CHIEFS) ▼

Traditionally, the *kgosi*, or chief, headed the *morafe*. All the members of the *morafe*, or chiefdom, owed allegiance to their chief. He held all the land in trust, distributing it to those under his authority.

The *kgosi* was not only responsible for ruling his people but was also a religious leader. He served as a vital link between the community and its ancestors. The *kgosi* was highly respected. Offensive behavior toward him was punishable by a sizable fine or even death.

The *kgosi*'s deeds were always praised by the people in special praise poems. He was closely

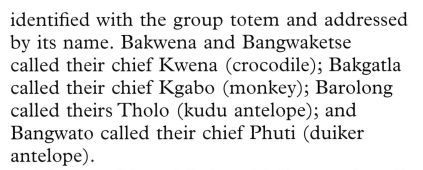

identified with the group totem and addressed by its name. Bakwena and Bangwaketse called their chief Kwena (crocodile); Bakgatla called their chief Kgabo (monkey); Barolong called theirs Tholo (kudu antelope); and Bangwato called their chief Phuti (duiker antelope).

The act of *bogosi* (being chief) was a hereditary birthright passed from father to son. Under the British administration of Botswana the system of inheriting power was changed, so that *dikgosi* could be nominated, elected, or appointed. This changed the Setswana view that a chief was a chief by right of his birth. The succession of women to *bogosi* occurred only when women ruled as regents until the rightful male heir took over.

The chief was helped and advised on the administration of the *morafe* by councillors, who were often his relatives. Below the councillors came the *dikgosana*, or headmen, who ruled areas far away from the main village, or *motse*. They were in turn assisted by local councillors, who were usually related to the headmen. These outlying areas were, and still are, divided into wards, which consist of about 100 family homesteads. Headmen were under the authority of the *kgosi*. Although the *kgosi* was the overall ruler of the *morafe*, he depended largely on the councillors and the headmen.

▼ *KGOTLA* ▼

Today, as in the past, the center of the *kgosi*'s administration is the *kgotla*, an assembly or court attended by each and every man. The *kgosi* presided over important meetings, legal cases, interviews with visitors, and ceremonies that were always held at the *kgotla*. Almost all important events, decisions, and deeds fell within his jurisdiction. The *kgotla* acted as an assembly for the entire *morafe*. Members could freely express their opinions regarding community affairs and could make decisions and laws. If the majority of the *kgotla* disagreed with the judgment of the *kgosi*, his ruling could be changed. This democratic tradition formed the basis for modern government in Botswana.

Traditionally, women were excluded from the *kgotla* unless they were specifically called to attend. This meant that all important positions within the traditional system of government were dominated by men. The *kgotla* continues to play a key role in the life of Batswana, although its judicial function has been replaced by modern courts for all but minor legal matters. Today women are not officially banned from the meetings, but men continue to dominate the *kgotla*. However, in governmental positions in Botswana and South Africa, women are now treated as equals.

The power of *dikgosi* declined during British rule. Today chiefs are all members of the House

Today Botswana is a modern country with large cities, where people hold a wide variety of jobs. In rural areas, however, many families continue to grow their own food as they did in the past. This woman is grinding grain for her family.

of Chiefs, which does not pass laws but advises the government by making recommendations. Although the House of Chiefs has no direct power, it is still very influential. This is because Batswana in rural areas still regard their chiefs as their leaders and direct representatives.

Botswana is now ruled by a parliament, which contains both members of the governing party and of the opposition. A president, advised by cabinet ministers, leads the government. In

Rural women tend their fields and run their homesteads. These women are pounding grain. The woman on the left fills the wooden mortar with grain, while the woman on the right pounds it with a heavy wooden pestle.

parliament, members debate social issues, pass laws, and ensure that government policy and administration are carried out. General elections must be held at least once every five years.

▼ ECONOMY ▼

In the past Botswana's economy centered around farming and herding animals. Batswana grew crops such as sorghum (a grain), sweet reed (like sugarcane), kidney beans, pumpkins,

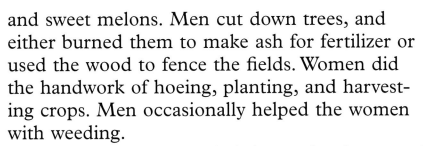

and sweet melons. Men cut down trees, and either burned them to make ash for fertilizer or used the wood to fence the fields. Women did the handwork of hoeing, planting, and harvesting crops. Men occasionally helped the women with weeding.

Men herded and tended the cattle, sheep, and goats. This job was considered as difficult as farming the fields. Young men were responsible for keeping the animals out of the cornfields. Skinning the animals, tanning their hides, and milking were duties also performed by men.

Cattle were regarded as the measure of a person's wealth and status. They also created and cemented social ties; a bride-price of cattle, called *bogadi*, had to be paid by a groom to the family of a bride. Cattle provided milk, meat, and clothing (from the hides). They could also be used in a loan system called *mafisa*. The *mafisa* system placed the poor in the service of those who had more cattle and were therefore wealthier. In return for looking after the cattle of a wealthy person, a poor person, or client, under the *mafisa* system was given food and lodging and paid one male calf per year. Over time a client could build up a small herd. The system was intended to close the gap between the rich and the poor and to improve understanding and cooperation between the different levels of society.

Women in Botswana make a variety of fine baskets, which are often sold along the roadside (above) to people who pass by.

In earlier times the economy of the Batswana was supplemented by hunting. Boys and men hunted with the help of dogs and wooden clubs called *dithobane*, which were also weapons of war.

Trade among Batswana groups and with other societies was an important aspect of the precolonial economy. Batswana traded cattle, grain, tools, and weapons. Oxen were regarded as more useful than cows because they were used for transportation and for pulling plows. A good ox could be traded for four cows.

Successful farmers who harvested more sorghum than others could trade their surplus. In times of famine or before the harvest season, a basket of corn could be worth one chicken or even one ox, depending on how severe the shortage of food was. Local blacksmiths traded weapons and farming tools for grain, sheep, and cows.

Batswana began to trade with Europeans in the 1840s. They sold animal skins, ivory, and ostrich feathers to Europeans in return for cutlery, beads, and trinkets. Plows, wagons, and guns were among the items obtained from Europeans that made Batswana farming and hunting easier.

The beef industry is still very important in Botswana. There are approximately 3 million cattle in Botswana compared with only 1.3 million people. Roughly 20 percent of the animals are owned by top officials and politicians. Although the beef industry is so significant, the national economy of Botswana is now dominated by the mineral industry, particularly diamond mining.▲

chapter

4

RELIGION AND CUSTOMS

THE RELIGION, CUSTOMS, AND TRADITIONS
of Batswana changed after contact with
Europeans. Christian missionaries discouraged
most Setswana customs. They rejected polygyny
(having more than one wife at the same time) as
sinful and ancestor worship as pagan. They dis-
approved of animal sacrifice as a way of making
contact with the spiritual world and replaced it
with prayer. They saw no value in traditional
medicine, which combined a thorough knowledge of healing plants and spiritual and psychological healing techniques.

They forced young people to choose between
going to initiation school, where they learned
Setswana customs, or to missionary schools,
where they received Western educations.
Setswana tradition was thus brought into conflict with Christianity and other Western values.
As more and more Batswana received Western

Some Batswana today combine Christianity with their own traditional beliefs. Both God and the ancestors are worshipped in what are called Africanist church groups. Seen above is a baptism held by one such group. To join the church, the candidate must be completely submerged three times—in the name of the Father, Son, and Holy Spirit.

education, the practice of Setswana traditions declined. However, many Batswana, particularly in rural areas, continue to follow traditional religious beliefs as well as other Setswana ways of life.

Before the influence of Christianity and Western religious customs, Batswana religion was practiced by performing communal and private religious ceremonies. Each ceremony occurred at special times and had specific rules and procedures that had to be followed. The practices discussed below reflect the people's beliefs and understanding of their world, the

43

universe, and themselves. The worldview of Batswana and their daily lives were both deeply religious.

▼ GOD AND THE ANCESTORS ▼

The Setswana name for God, or the Supreme Being, is Modimo. In traditional belief, Modimo is far too great to be directly addressed by mortals. Only after the missionaries came did Batswana begin to address the Supreme Being directly as Christians do.

Traditionally, the people communicate with their deceased relatives, or ancestors. Known as *badimo*, the ancestors act as the go-betweens for the living family and Modimo. They are regarded as the ever-present guardians of their living relatives. In return, the living relatives must perform various ceremonies and sacrifices.

However, the ancestors can be easily upset if their living kin do not show them the proper respect. In the past, for example, before drinking beer or eating meals on important occasions, some food or drink was placed on the ground to feed *badimo*, who are believed to live in the earth. The first crop during harvesttime could not be eaten until the *kgosi* tasted the "first fruits" and gave some of the harvest to *badimo* as an offering of thanks. Certain animals, particularly all-black and all-white ones, were reserved as sacrifices to *badimo*.

Even in times of danger and desperation, such as epidemics, war, famine, and drought, Modimo was not directly addressed. Instead the *kgosi* was required to perform special ceremonies for his people.

▼ RAINMAKING ▼

Batswana believed that offending the *badimo* caused drought. The *kgosi* and his *baroka* (priests) had the responsibility of making amends to *badimo*. Rainmaking was one of the most important duties of chiefs in the past, since the well-being of the whole community depended on rain. Each Batswana group had its own particular ceremonies for rain.

In some cases a special cow called *kope* (from the Setswana word *kopa*, meaning to ask) was sacrificed to the ancestors to ask for rain. It was usually a pure black or pure white cow. The *kgosi* and *baroka* mixed the cow's blood with herbs, went to a sacred place, and used a branch to sprinkle the mixture throughout the countryside. Rain clouds were expected to gather within a few days.

Sometimes the rainmaking ceremony took place near the *kgotla*. The *kgosi* assigned regiments to build an enclosure of thorny branches. The center of the cattle kraal, or corral, was then cleared, a fireplace was built, and the area was swept and plastered with clay or cow dung.

The *kgosi* and his trusted *baroka* entered the holy place. A mixture of herbs was burned continuously for several days, and smoke curled up toward the sky to bring rain. If it did not rain, it was a sign that *badimo* were not yet satisfied, and the process would be repeated.

▼ *BOLOI* (WITCHCRAFT) AND ▼ DIVINATION

Batswana believed that individuals and families had to be protected against witches, or *baloi* (singular: *moloi*), who could use herbs and spiritual power to bewitch people. Newborn children were immediately given protective treatment by a diviner, someone who combined spiritual power with the knowledge of herbs.

Witches were thought to be motivated largely by jealousy. In the dead of the night, witches roamed the countryside nude. Their magical powers could open locked doors and transform a sleeper into an animal on which the witch could ride. Witches could also poison and even kill their victims.

There was, and still is, a popular belief that some witches or evil diviners could be paid to direct lightning to strike at houses, people, or cattle. Anyone found guilty of *boloi*, or witchcraft, could be put to death.

Whenever someone fell ill, a diviner cast his set of divining bones on the ground and

Diviners, or traditional healers, continue to be consulted by many Batswana today. To diagnose the causes of physical, psychological, and spiritual problems, and to prescribe cures, diviners "throw the bones." The bones are a set of divination articles, which usually includes small bones, shells, seeds, and other items. The diviner bases his advice on the meaning he reads in the way that the bones have fallen (above).

diagnosed the problem from the pattern they made. He then applied herbs to cuts made on the patient's body. These strengthened the patient and protected him or her against evil spirits. The diviner's payment was usually a goat, a sheep, or a cow, depending on the severity of the illness.

▼ INITIATION ▼

In the past, when Batswana boys and girls reached puberty, they were expected to enter

47

In the past, young Batswana men had to attend initiation schools, where they were prepared for adult life and trained to be warriors. Today initiation is rare. Young men prepare for their future by attending school. Instead of competing as warriors, they play sports.

separate initiation schools: *bogwera* for boys and *bojale* for girls. The influence of missionaries and Western-educated Batswana leaders discouraged initiation. Today initiation ceremonies are almost nonexistent except among the Bakgatla.

Over a period of about three months, elders and diviners taught them all about significant Setswana traditions and customs as well as the duties of their gender. Each initiation school, male or female, formed a *mophato*, or regiment,

of peers who remained closely connected to each other throughout their lives.

Boys underwent rigorous training to turn them into disciplined warriors. Flogging the initiates, who were known as *magwane* (the raw ones), was accepted as a toughening exercise. They had to live in the bush and hunt and kill animals for food. They were instructed on the duties of being the head of a family and contributing to the *morafe*. They had to learn by heart praise songs for famous chiefs, ancestors, and headmen. They practiced what were considered male skills, including carpentry, sewing karosses (cloaks made of hides), shield making, and various male dances.

At the end of their time at initiation school, the boys were circumcised and finally considered men. Circumcision was regarded as an important step from boyhood to manhood.

They then returned to the *kgotla* for their graduation ceremony. The *kgosi* gave them a regimental name, often one that reflected some current event. From then on, the men in this regiment, consisting of those similar in age, were closely bonded together and would assist each other in times of need.

Girls' initiation ceremonies were held at the same time but in a different location. Girl initiates usually wore skin skirts and wrapped the upper part of their bodies with thin sticks.

These were very uncomfortable and taught women to bear discomfort. Their faces were painted with *letsoku* (clay). They were taught the traditional female roles in raising children and running the household.

Their graduation was held at *kgosing*, the chief's courtyard. There they received their regimental names. Female regiments could be called upon by the *kgosi* to perform certain tasks, such as replastering his walls and floors or cooking food and brewing beer for feasts.

Initiation enabled young people to be integrated into society as adults. Young men could now join the *kgotla* discussions and learn the art of being wise judges of community matters. Women could now marry and become responsible wives and mothers.

▼ MARRIAGE CUSTOMS ▼

Before the presence of Europeans, the Batswana society believed that many wives brought a man wealth and prosperity. Polygyny, a practice in which a man has more than one wife, resulted in large families. As a result, the family workforce was more productive.

The *kgosi* was the richest man in the society; he had more wives than most of his subjects. Councillors and the wealthy could afford many wives, but ordinary men could afford only two or three.

During a traditional wedding, the bride's female relatives and other women from the community form a procession (above). They accompany the bride to the groom's home.

The *kgosi*'s first wife was known as *mosadi yo motona*, the great wife, since her eldest son became the chief's heir. All other wives were junior to her. The *kgosi* and his siblings married within the royal family, so marriage among cousins was customary in the Batswana royal families.

In ordinary families, the boy's parents chose his bride based on the good name and reputation of the girl's family. Boys had to accept their parents' choice, but sometimes the boy could give his elder brother or uncle hints about his desire to marry a certain woman. Depending on the status of the woman's family, the man's family could agree or disagree.

To make a marriage contract, a boy's family made a visit to the girl's family that was known as *go kopa sego sa metsi*, which means to ask for a gourd of water. After this water had been given, the boy's family was expected to pay *bogadi*, a bride-price set in cattle. Five to eight head of cattle was the normal bride-price.

Cattle were slaughtered for the wedding feast. Before the bride could officially go to her new home at her in-laws' homestead, a group of elderly women called her aside. In a secret session, they briefed her on how to cope with the problems of marriage and childbirth.

Each wife had her own household and her own property—including cattle and fields— that were later inherited by her children. During the plowing season, a man's wives and children had to help clear bushes and hoe and plant the fields. The field preparation progressed according to rank: first the man's field, then the first wife's, and then those of his junior wives.

Meals were prepared inside each of the wives' households and presented to the husband, who usually enjoyed the variety of dishes in the company of relatives. It was taboo, or *moila*, for men to hang around the cooking fires of women.

Young Batswana children in rural areas still sometimes wear beaded aprons (above).

Polygyny could cause tensions. Jealousy among wives was not uncommon. Envy and witchcraft then haunted the family, resulting in many quarrels. The children of a polygynous family were often unsure of their position, because it depended to a large extent on the relationship between their father and his many wives. Children of a favorite wife believed that they were most favored by their father and tended to look down upon the other children in the household.

▼ BIRTHS ▼

The Batswana treated births, deaths, and burials with great respect. Since these were powerfully spiritual events, people performed special actions and ceremonies to mark these occasions.

Six months into a wife's pregnancy, her husband stopped sharing her room. He was regarded as being in a spiritually charged and potent state. Before he could take part in national events, such as hunting expeditions and other regimental duties, he had to undergo a ceremonial cleansing to prevent his potency from causing his comrades misfortune.

Immediately before the birth of his child, the husband usually took a long trip. A messenger was then sent to inform him of the birth. Even then the husband could not visit the wife or her house to see the child. Usually he waited about three months and underwent a special cleansing before visiting his wife and child.

During this time the mother was confined to her house and helped by her relatives. Before she and the baby could go outside into public view, they had to be ceremonially cleansed by a diviner.

▼ DEATH ▼

Today, as in the past, Batswana view death with great sorrow. Women express grief by

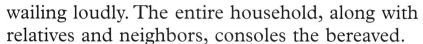

wailing loudly. The entire household, along with relatives and neighbors, consoles the bereaved.

According to tradition, at death a person's spirit begins the journey from the world of the living to the world of the dead. Since deceased relatives, or ancestors, look after their living relatives, every effort is made to ensure that all people are given proper burial. Particular ceremonies must also be performed to prepare the dead person for the spirit world.

Traditionally, men dug a grave in the cattle kraal or behind the household. The body was then wrapped in cowhide and buried in a sitting position so that it could stand up easily to join the ancestors. Diviners sprinkled herbs over the grave. Branches were placed on top of graves to prevent desecration and to keep witches away. Graves were regarded as sacred places not to be stepped upon.

The *kgosi* was buried in the *kgotla*; men were buried in their cattle kraals. Women were generally buried at the back of the homestead, but the Batlokwa people buried their women in the domestic courtyard, called the *lelwapa*.

Today, as a result of Western influence, villages and towns have one common cemetery for all, and people are buried in coffins. But the dead are still treated with great respect, and a cow is normally sacrificed to mark the event.▲

chapter

5

BOTSWANA TODAY

IN 1996 BOTSWANA CELEBRATED THIRTY years of independence. Its stability, harmony, and economic growth have made it outstanding among African countries.

▼ RURAL AND URBAN LIFE TODAY ▼

Although Botswana's economy is doing very well, there are still pockets of poverty in both the urban and rural areas. Many rural families are poor and have few opportunities or social services, such as health care.

The Botswana government has placed much emphasis on improving rural life and encouraging development. One program encourages villagers to improve their communities during times when no farming can be done. This program is called Ipelegeng, meaning self-reliance.

The Botswana government is working to improve conditions in rural areas (above).

Other programs assist in establishing job opportunities in rural areas and improving services such as roads and utilities.

Since its independence, Botswana's cities—particularly Gaborone and Francistown—have grown rapidly. Gaborone, the capital city, is one of the fastest growing cities in Africa. Urban areas have very good communication systems, transportation networks, water and electric services, and medical and educational facilities. However, city life is expensive, and urban dwellers must have a good income to support a largely Westernized lifestyle. City dwellers' incomes come from the same range of

The annual Independence Day celebration (above) provides an opportunity for people to celebrate both their cultural traditions and their achievements as a modern country. These boys perform a traditional dance.

occupations that are found in most other cities of the world.

Because city life seems to offer chances for higher income, many rural people move to the cities in the hopes of finding good jobs. However, many remain unemployed or find only low-paying jobs. These people make up the large population of the urban poor, who live in shantytowns and squatter camps on the edges of cities and towns. These settlements generally

Sir Ketumile Masire (above), president of Botswana, is proud of his country's democratic tradition and is optimistic about its future.

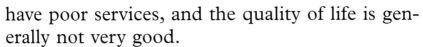

have poor services, and the quality of life is generally not very good.

The discovery of rich mineral deposits in the 1970s generated the income to develop and improve Botswana's economy. Since 1993 economic growth has slowed. This is due to a complex mix of factors, including drought, lower diamond prices, bureaucratic inefficiency, and downturns in other countries' economies.

Now that South Africa has introduced a democratic system and there is greater peace in the region, it is hoped that Botswana's economy will pick up again. However, some fear that South Africa may become a strong competitor, attracting investors away from Botswana.

Sir Ketumile Masire, president of Botswana, takes the opposite view. "We definitely welcome a new South Africa," he says. "While it will present a formidable challenge in attracting new investment, we think Botswana can still develop its own riches [alongside the other countries in the] subcontinent. The strong challenge should act only to bring out the best in us."▲

Glossary

ancestor worship Belief that the spirits of ancestors have power over the living.

apartheid Government system based on controlling people by keeping them in separate racial groups.

badimo Ancestral spirits.

baroka Priests.

bogadi Bride-price paid in cattle.

bogwera Men's initiation.

bojale Women's initiation.

boloi Witchcraft.

diviner One who can see future events through supernatural powers.

kgosi **(plural:** *dikgosi***)** Chief.

kgotla Traditional assembly or meeting; meeting place.

kope Cow sacrificed during a rainmaking ceremony.

mafisa A system of lending cattle to the poor.

moila Taboo; something forbidden.

moloi **(plural:** *baloi***)** Witch.

morafe **(plural:** *merafe***)** Chiefdom; ethnic subgroup.

motse Village.

totem An emblem that unites people who are descended from the same ancestors.

For Further Reading

Balfour, Daryl and Sharna. *This is Botswana.*
Gaborone: Pula Press, 1994.

Bond, C., Johnston, P. and Bannister, A.
Okavango: Sea of Land: Land of Water.
Gaborone: Pula Press, 1977.

Botswana: Visitors' Guide. Gaborone: Department
of Information and Broadcasting, 1994.

Ramsay, Jeff and Morton, Fred. *The Birth of
Botswana: A History of the Bechuanaland
Protectorate from 1910 to 1966.* Gaborone:
Longman, 1987.

Social Studies Books 5 and 6. Gaborone: Macmillan Publishing Company (Pty) Ltd., 1990.

Tlou, Thomas and Campbell, Alec. *History of
Botswana.* Gaborone: Macmillan Publishing
Company (Pty) Ltd., 1984.

Index

A
AAC (African Advisory Council), 27, 29
ancestor worship, 15, 42, 44, 54
apartheid, 9, 30–31

B
Bakwena Chiefdom, 15, 23, 25, 26, 35
Bechuanaland Protectorate, 10, 25, 26, 27, 30
birth, 54
Boers, 24–26
Bophuthatswana, 9, 25, 30–32
bride-price (*bogadi*), 39, 52
BSAC (British South Africa Company), 25–26

C
cattle
    as food, 21, 39
    as religious sacrifices, 45–46, 55
    as wealth, 14, 16, 39, 52
Cape Town, 19, 26, 27
Christianity, 24, 42, 43, 44

D
death, 54–55
Difaqane, 21, 23
divination, 46–47, 54, 55
Dutch, 19, 24

E
economy, Botswana, 17, 38–41, 56, 60
education, 24, 42–43, 48

F
farming, 38–39, 41, 52, 56

G
gender roles, 35, 39, 47–50, 52
Great Britain, 19, 24, 25–26, 27–29

H
herding and hunting, 16, 38, 40, 54
House of Chiefs, 36–37
housing, 17–18, 58

I
initiation schools, 42, 47–50

K
Kalahari Desert, 12, 20
kgosi (chief), 24, 27, 29, 34–35, 36, 44–45, 49, 50, 51, 55
kgotla (meeting place), 35, 36, 49, 50, 55

L
Livingstone, David, 23, 25
LMS (London Missionary Society), 21, 23, 25

M
marriage, 50–52
merafe (chiefdoms), 15–16, 23, 34, 35, 49
missionaries, 20, 21, 23–24, 34, 42, 44, 48
Moffat, Robert, 21, 23

Mzilikazi (Ndebele leader), 21, 23, 26

N
Namibia, 10, 32

P
polygyny, 42, 50, 53
praise poems and songs, 34, 49

R
Rhodes, Cecil, 25–27

S
Setswana (language and customs), 9–10, 16, 23, 24, 35, 42–43, 48

South Africa, 9, 10, 21, 27, 30–32, 36, 60

T
totems, 15–16, 35
trade, 19–20, 32, 40–41
Transvaal, Republic of, 24, 26–27

W
witchcraft, 46–47

Z
Zimbabwe, 10, 26, 32

ABOUT THE AUTHORS

Born in Botswana, Maitseo M. Bolaane earned her Master's degree in African History at the School of Oriental and African Studies (SOAS), University of London. Currently a lecturer in the History Department at the University of Botswana, she is also involved in the University of Botswana's Basarwa Research Project.

Part T. Mgadla, also born in Botswana, holds a Ph.D. in History from Boston University. He is currently a senior lecturer in the History Department at the University of Botswana. He has published several articles on the history of Botswana, and recently co-authored *Building a Nation* (Longman, 1996), a book on Botswana.

PHOTO CREDITS

All photos by Jean Morris © McGregor Museum, Kimberley, South Africa, except: cover © Batswanacraft Marketing Company (Pty) Ltd. and p. 13 top and bottom © Dept. of Wildlife and National Parks, Botswana, courtesy of Dept. of Tourism, Botswana; p. 22 courtesy of the South African Library, Cape Town; p. 57 by Bruce Paton © Impact Visuals; p. 58 by Catherine Smith © Impact Visuals; p. 59 by Orde Eliason © Impact Visuals.

CONSULTING EDITOR AND LAYOUT

Gary N. van Wyk, Ph.D.

SERIES DESIGN

Kim Sonsky